ROBERT WINN
HIGH PERFORMANCE FLUTE
THE SEQUEL

Grade 5 onwards

FREE CD
WITH 30 DUETS FOR DOWNLOAD (PDF)

AMA
VERLAG

Impressum

All titles: Copyright © 2017 by AMA Musikverlag

Alle Rechte vorbehalten
Copyright © 2017 by
AMA Verlag GmbH
Postfach 1168
50301 Brühl
Germany

http://www.ama-verlag.de
e-Mail: mail@ama-verlag.de

Umschlagsgestaltung: Kotronis
Gesamtherstellung: Detlef Kessler
Printed in Germany

AMA 610168
ISMN M-50155-101-9
ISBN 978-3-89922-193-0

All rights reserved
Copyright © 2017 by
AMA Verlag GmbH
P.O. Box 1168
50301 Bruehl
Germany

http:/www.ama-verlag.de
e-Mail: mail@ama-verlag.de

Cover design: Kotronis
Overall production: Detlef Kessler
Printed in Germany

AMA 610168
ISMN M-50155-101-9
ISBN 978-3-89922-193-0

Foreword

Thanks to the overwhelming success of High Performance Flute, THE SEQUEL, is a new look at the repertoire for grade 5 and onwards. Once again studies and accompanied flute pieces form the basis with additional duet material and many complete works to enhance the learning experience. Where practical I have simplified the piano parts, to encourage young people playing together.

Thanks to Brigitte Windolph at AMA who's patience and insight are invaluable and to my wonderful wife Gülçe, without whom none of this would be possible.

Vorwort

Dank des überwältigenden Erfolgs von „High Performance Flute", bietet THE SEQUEL einen neuen Blick auf das Repertoire für Flöte ab Grade 5. Auch hier bilden Studien und begleitete Stücke für Flöte die Grundlage der Schule mit zusätzlichem Duomaterial und viele komplette Stücke, um die Vielfalt des Unterrichts zu ergänzen. Soweit möglich, habe ich die Piano-Parts vereinfacht, um das Zusammenspiel zu erleichtern.

Dank an Brigitte Windolph vom AMA Verlag, deren Geduld und Einsicht von unschätzbarem Wert sind, und an meine wunderbare Frau Gülçe, ohne die dieses ganze Projekt nicht möglich gewesen wäre.

Contents / Inhalt

Daily Exercises

Tägliche Übungen

*Sing a comfortable note,
find this note on your flute!*

*Singe eine Note, die dir leicht fällt und finde diese
Note auf deiner Flöte.*

Play a long note and sing a scale with it!

Spiele eine lange Note und singe dazu eine Skala!

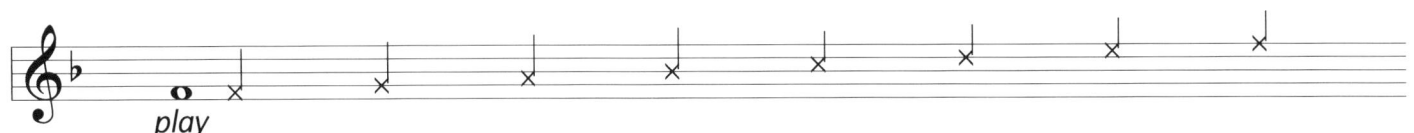

Sing a long note and play a scale with it!

Singe eine lange Note und spiele dazu eine Skala!

*Hold a long note and glissando up and down
with the voice!*

*Halte eine lange Note und singe ein Glissando
auf- und abwärts!*

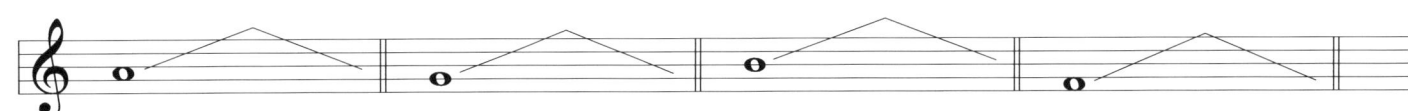

etc.

FRÈRE JACQUES! *Sing + play together!*

Singe + spiele gleichzeitig!

Aquarium *(from Le Carneval des animaux)*

C. Saint-Saëns

Register Changes / Oktavwechsel

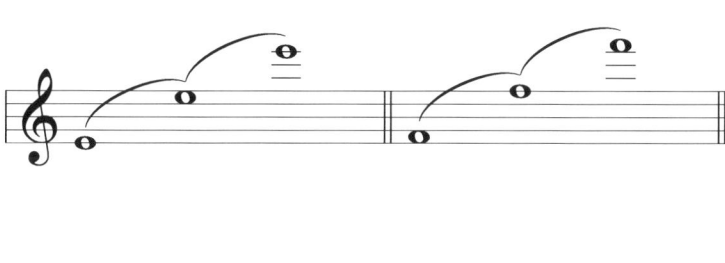

○ = Harmonic notes created by increasing the
     wind speed using the same fingering
  = Obertöne durch einen verstärkten Luftstrom
     bei gleicher Griffweise

etc.

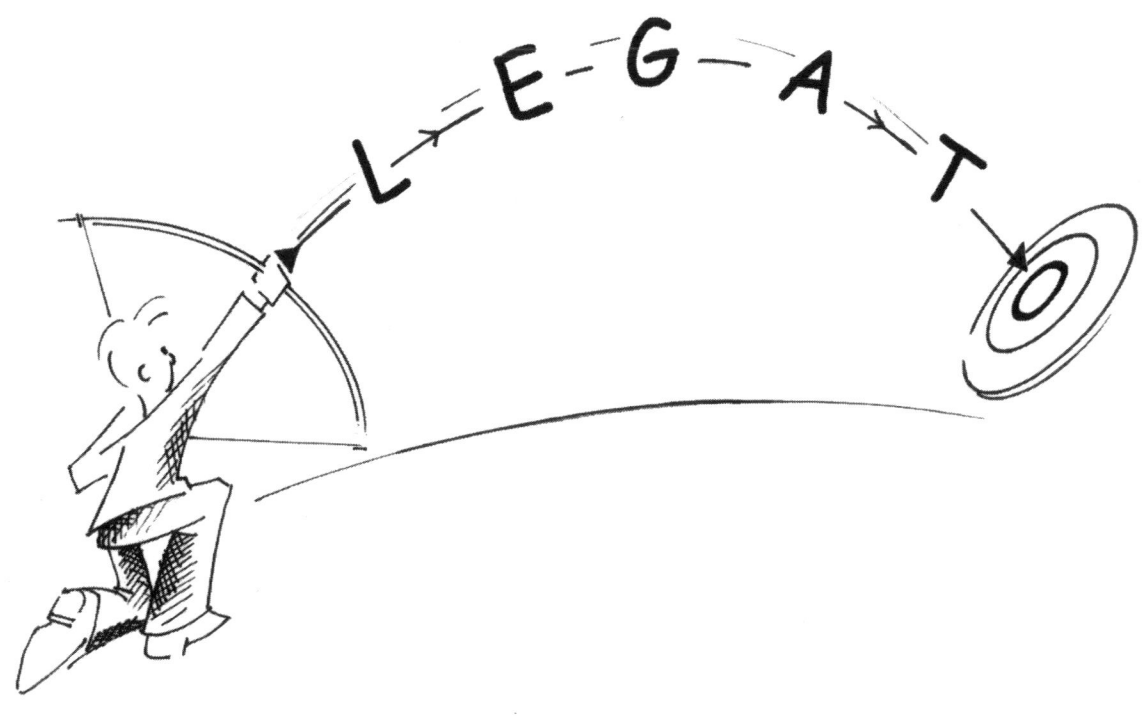

L-E-G-A-T

Sonata A Minor

Piano – page 12 / Duos

A. Corelli (Op. 5, No. 8)
Arr.: R. Winn

PRELUDIO

Largo

ALLEMANDE

Allegro moderato

Boléro

M. Ravel

Étude in C Major

G. Gariboldi

Ah! So Pure (Martha)

Piano – page 60

Fr. von Flotow
Arr. R. Winn

11

Salut d'Amour

Piano – page 3

E. Elgar, Op. 12

Étude

L. Drouet (25 Studies, No. 16)

13

Intermezzo (from Cavalleria Rusticana)

Piano – page 63

P. Mascagni
Arr.: R. Winn

Étude

J. Andersen (Op. 41)

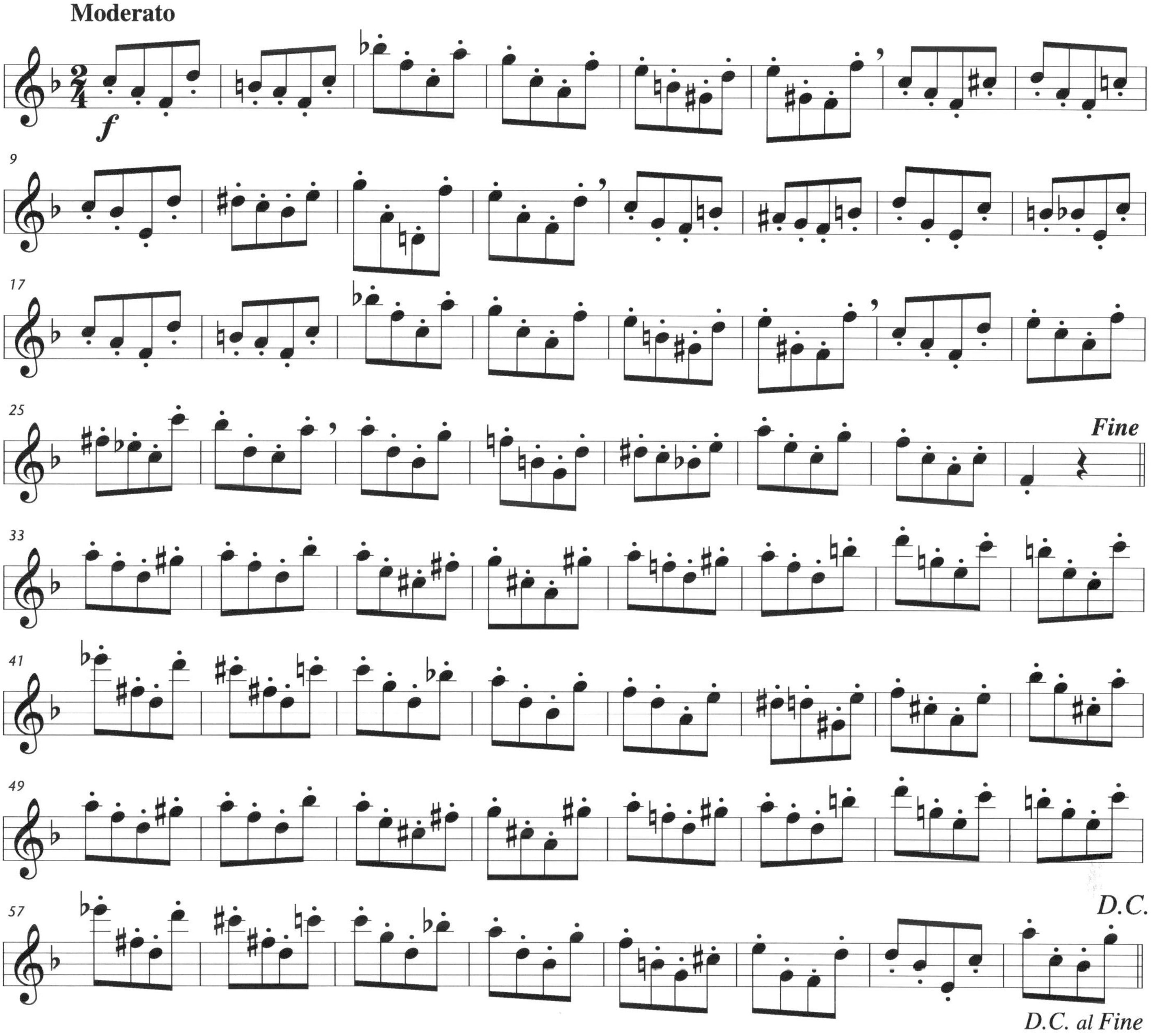

Moderato

Arkansas Traveller (Country Dance)

Trad.

Song of India (from the Legend "Sadko")

Piano – page 52

N. Rimsky-Korsakoff

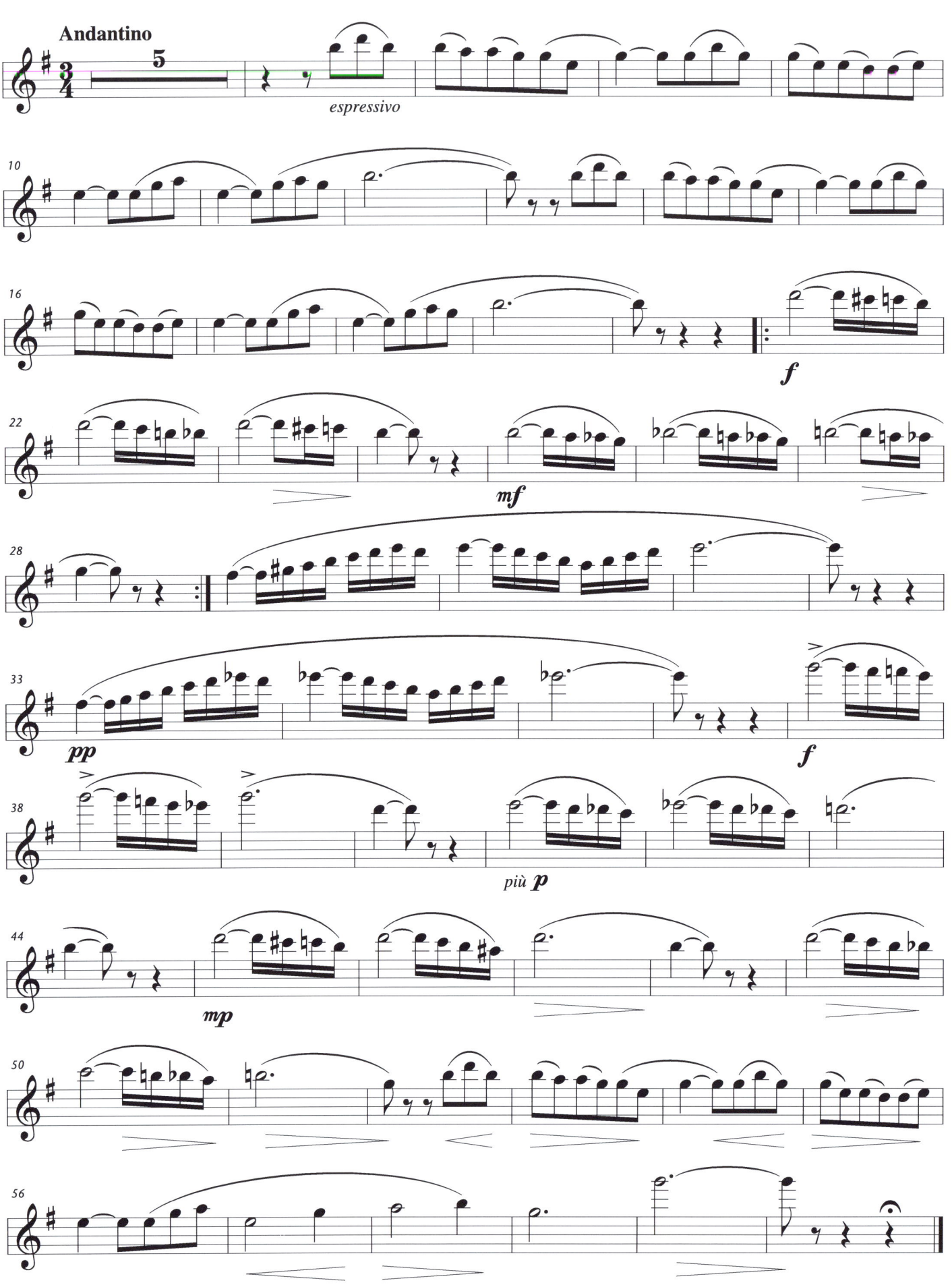

Étude

J. Andersen (Op. 37, No. 6)

Élégie

J. Massenet (Op. 10)

Fantasia No. 10

G. Ph. Telemann

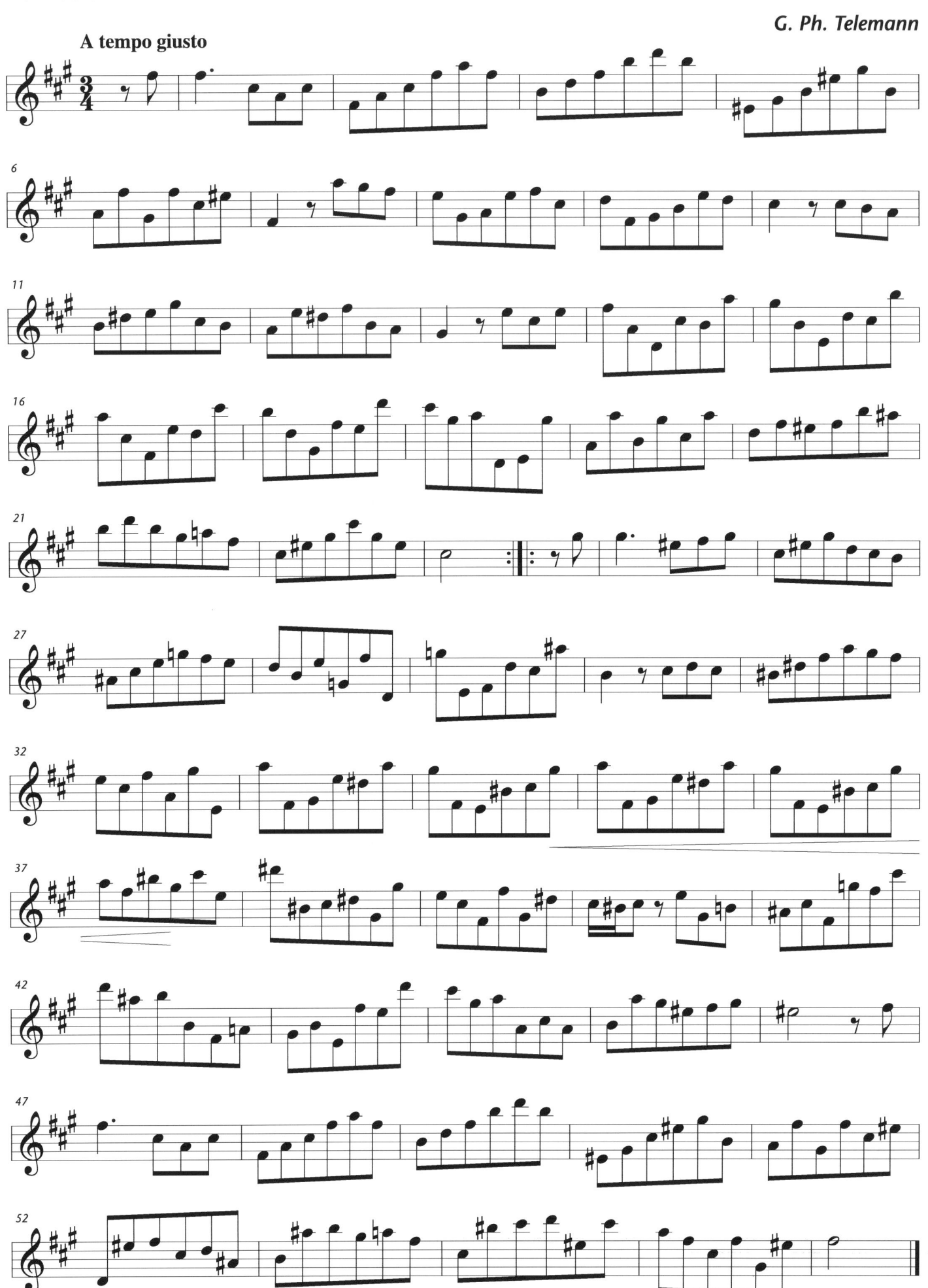

Étude

J. Andersen (Op. 37, No.7)

Étude

J. Andersen (Op. 41, No. 2)

Aria (from Lucia di Lammermoor)

G. Donizetti

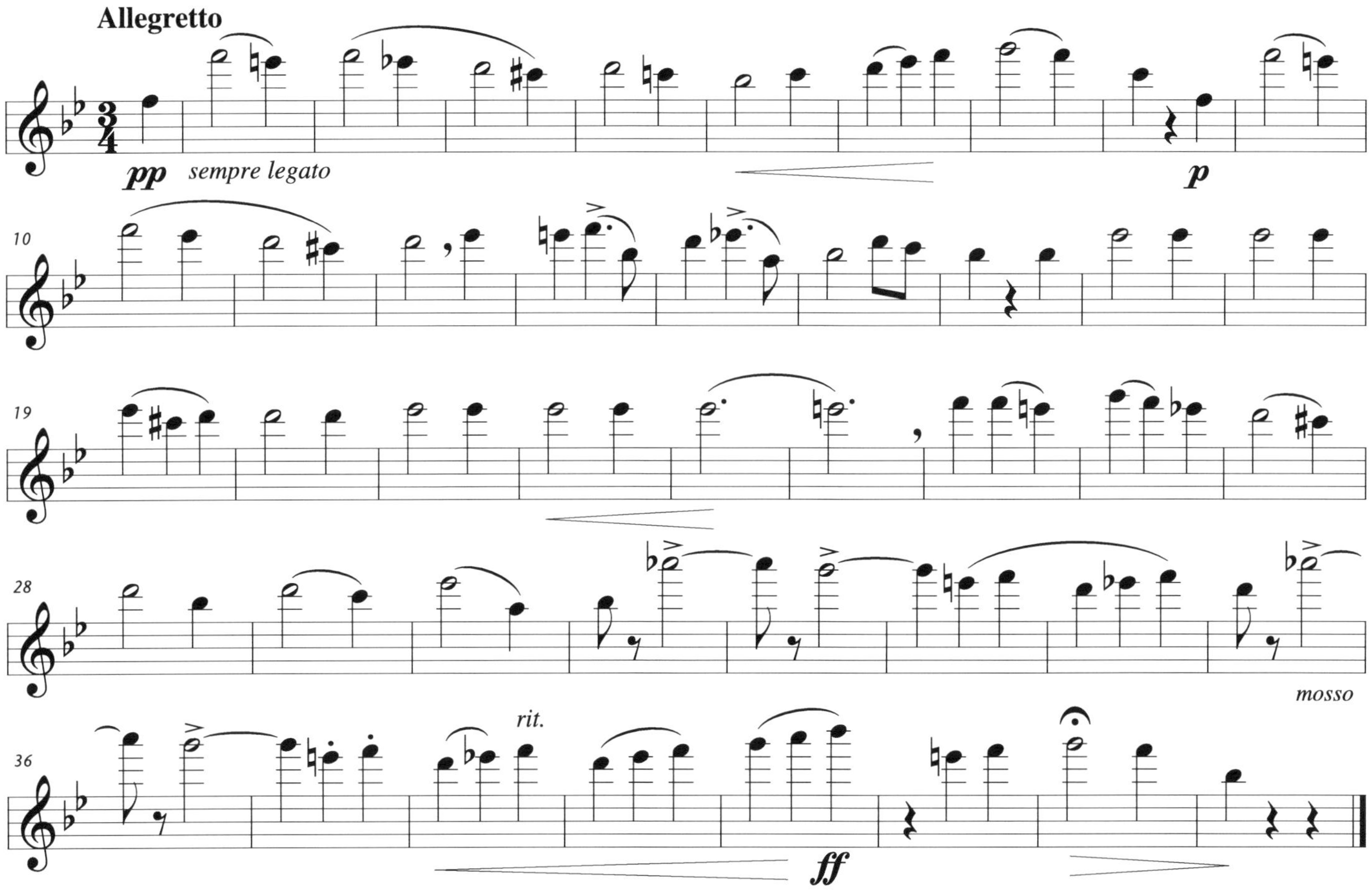

Tambourin

Piano – page 16

F.-J. Gossec

Nabucco Swing

G. Verdi
Arr.: R. Winn

play the quavers

Allegro

Étude

E. Köhler (Op. 33)

Allegretto

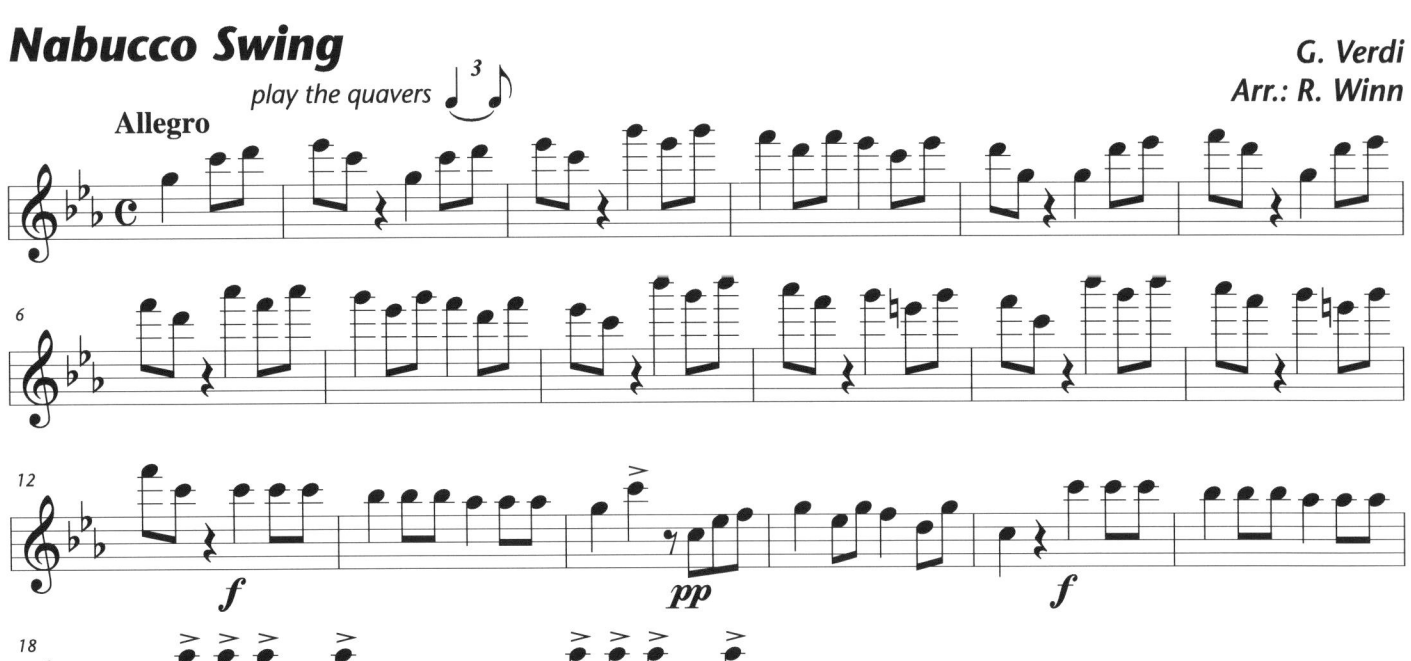

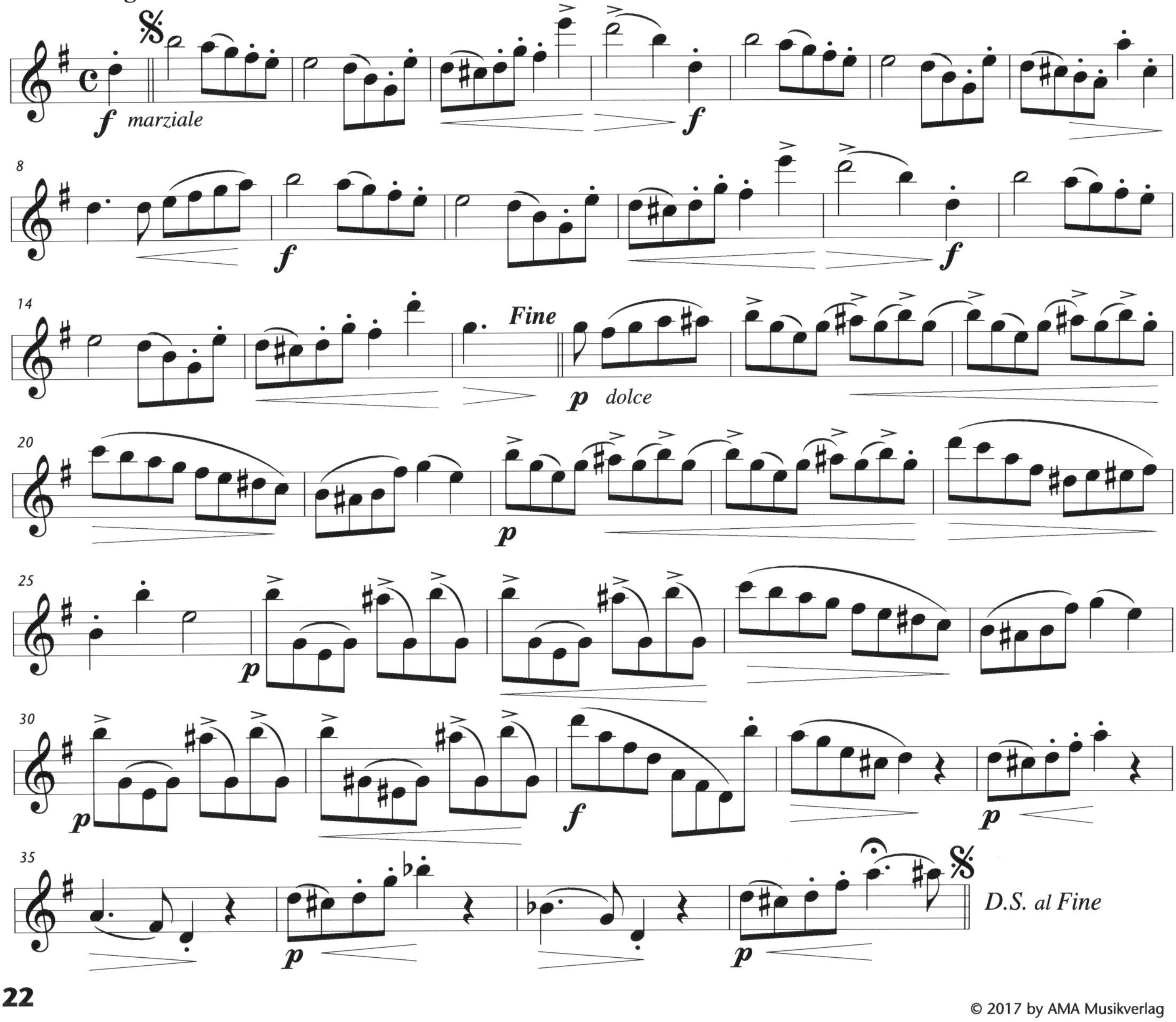

Meditation From Thaïs

Piano – page 88

J. Massenet
Arr.: R. Winn

Pavane

Duos

G. Fauré

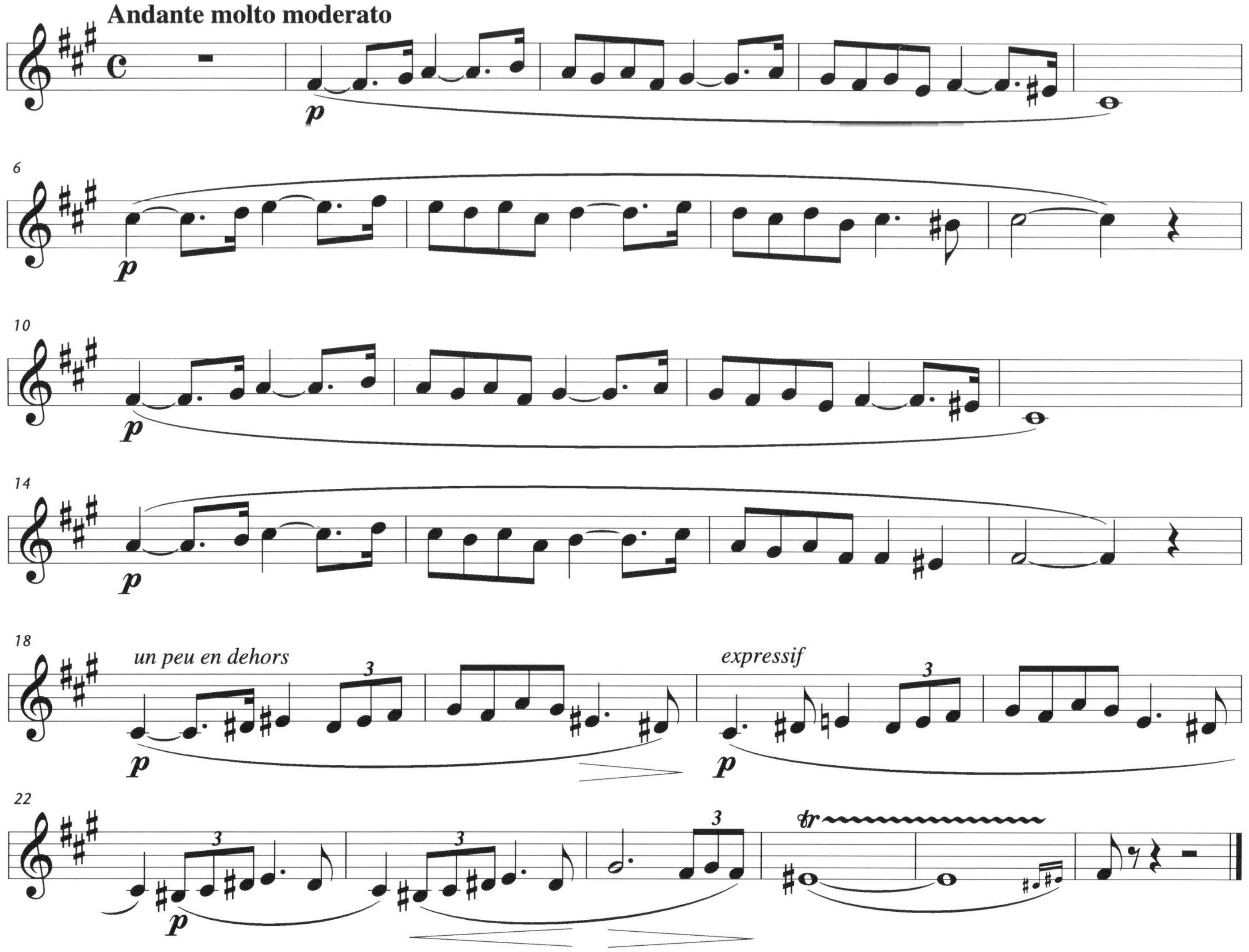
Andante molto moderato
p
6
10
14
18
un peu en dehors
3
expressif
22
tr

Songs Without Words

F. Mendelssohn-Bartholdy (Op. 109)

Andante
5
9
13

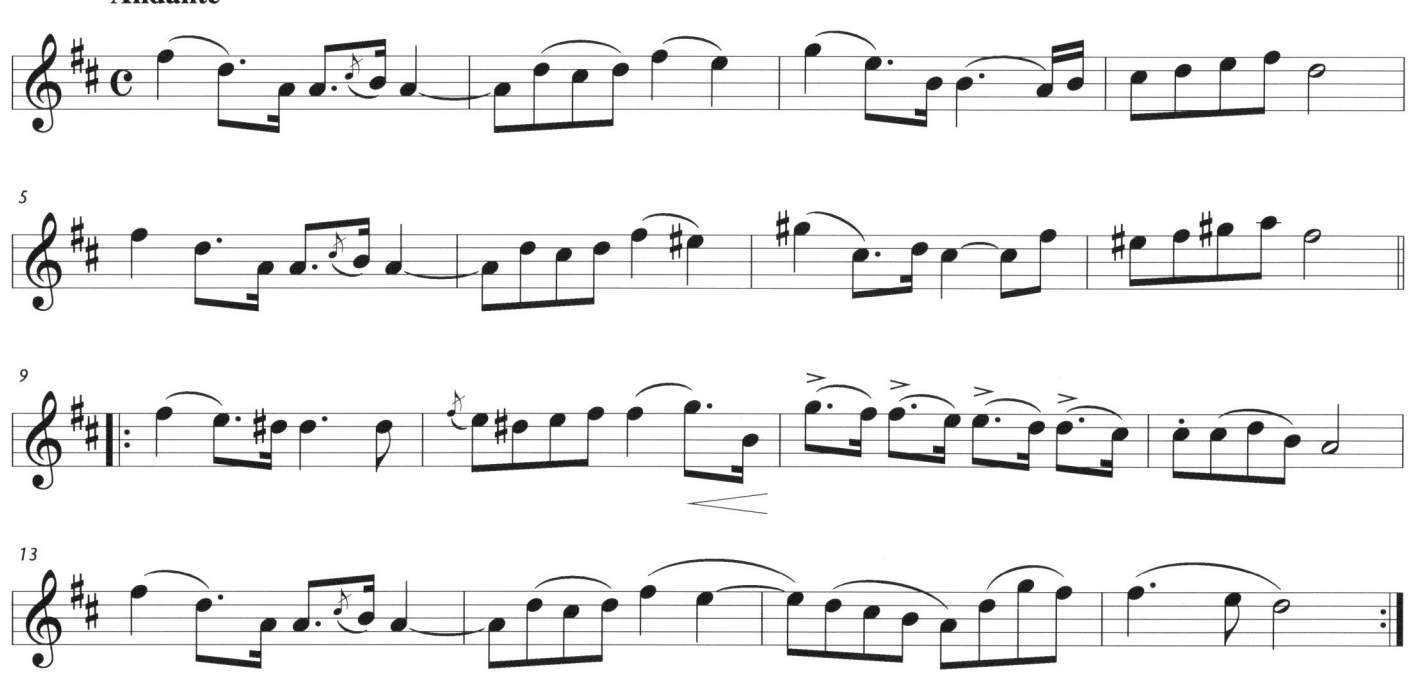

Étude

J. Andersen (Op. 41, No. 8)

Adagio from Flute Quartet

Piano – page 55

W. A. Mozart (KV 285)
Arr.: R. Winn

March of the Toy Soldiers (Nutcracker Suite)

P. I. Tchaikovsky

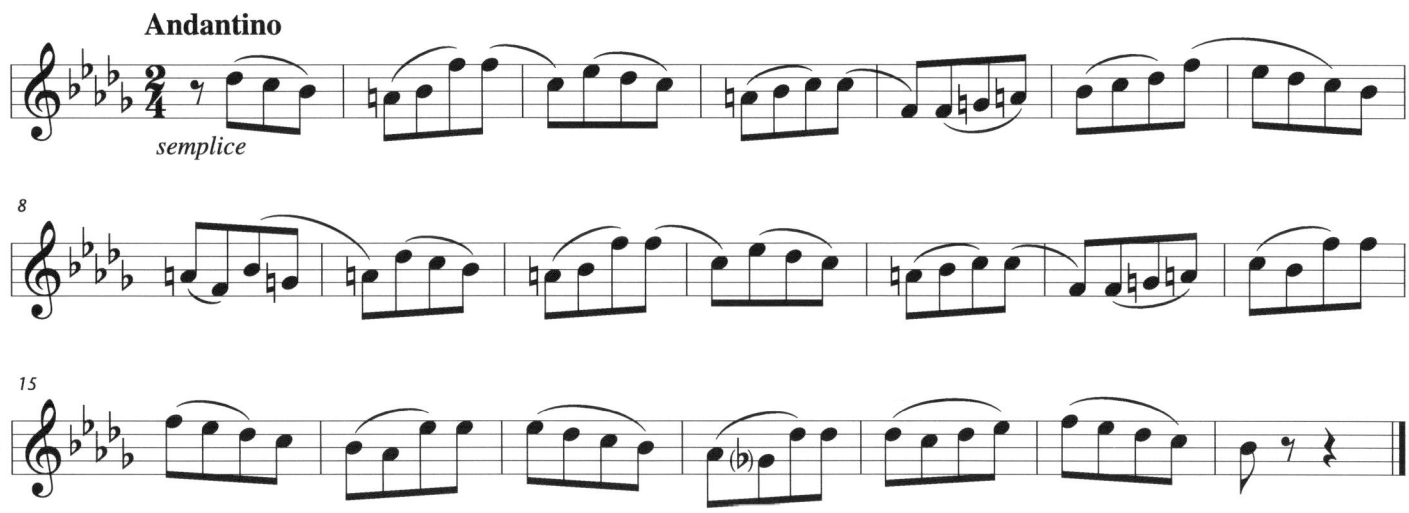

4th Symphony II

P. I. Tchaikowsky

Frühlingsstimmen-Walzer

Piano – page 26

Joh. Strauss
Arr.: R. Winn

Tempo di valse

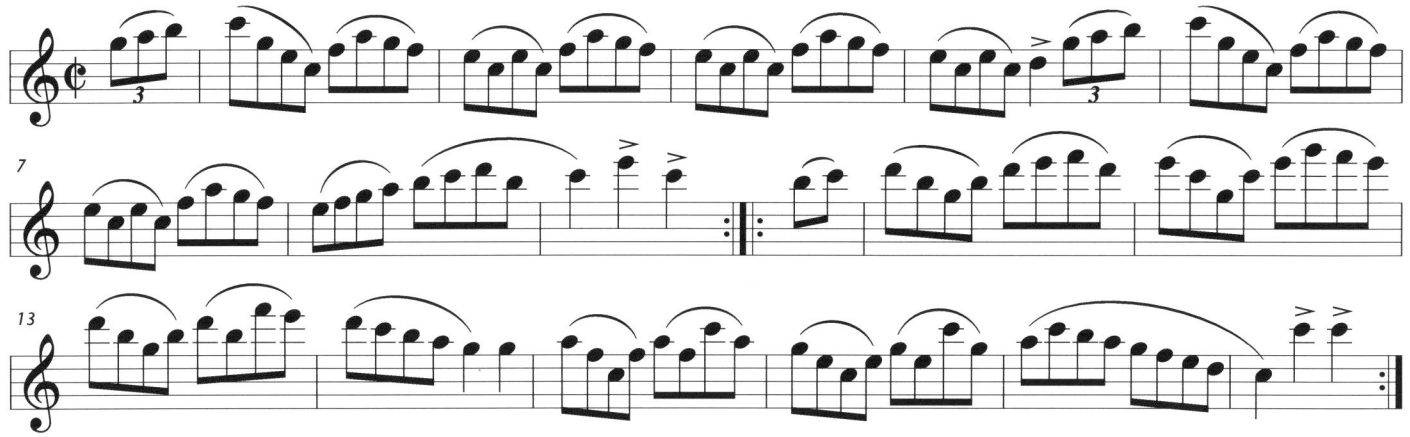

Fischer's Hornpipe

Trad.

Étude

E. Köhler

Romance

Piano – page 32

C. Saint-Saëns (Op. 37)

30

Vocalise

Piano – page 68

S. Rachmaninoff (Op. 34, No. 14)

Lentamente molto cantabile

Étude

E. Köhler (Op. 33, No. 8)

Waltz of the Flowers (Nutcracker Suite)

Piano – page 24

P. I. Tschaikovsky
Arr.: R. Winn

Por una Cabeza

C. Gardel

Trumpet Concerto – Allegro Rondo

J. N. Hummel

35

Madrigal

Piano – page 72

Ph. Gaubert

Moderato quasi Allegretto

un peu plus vite

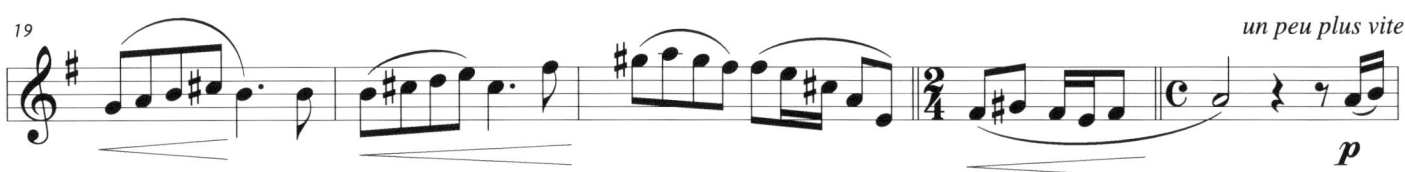

a tempo

poco animato   *rit.*

a tempo

36

Fantasy on Rigoletto

Piano – page 20

G. Verdi
Arr.: Fr. & K. Doppler

Étude

Allegro moderato

J. Demersseman

La forza del destino

G. Verdi

Boléro

M. Ravel

Nessun dorma

G. Puccini

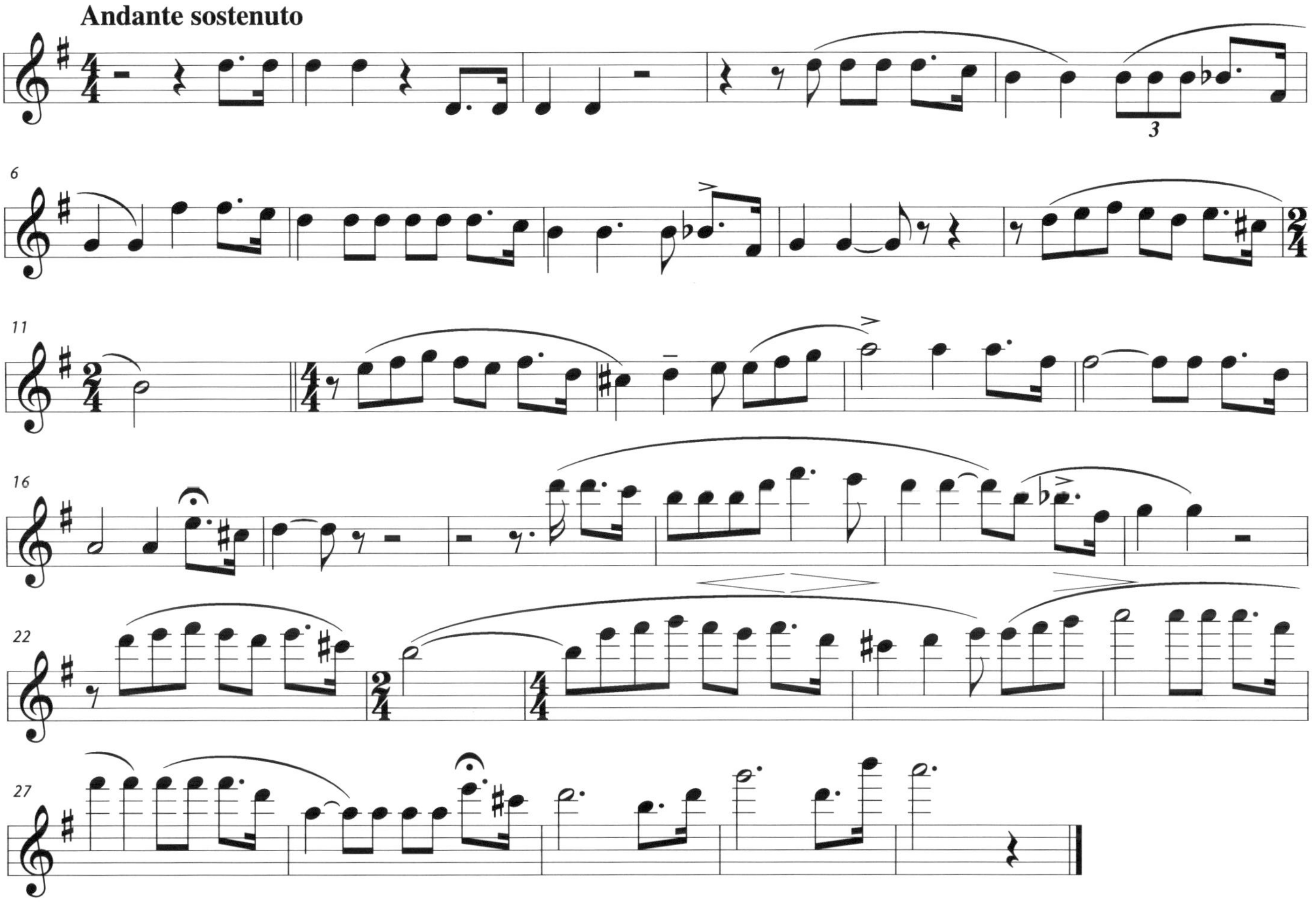
Andante sostenuto

Étude

L. Drouet

Allegro
f
cresc.
mf

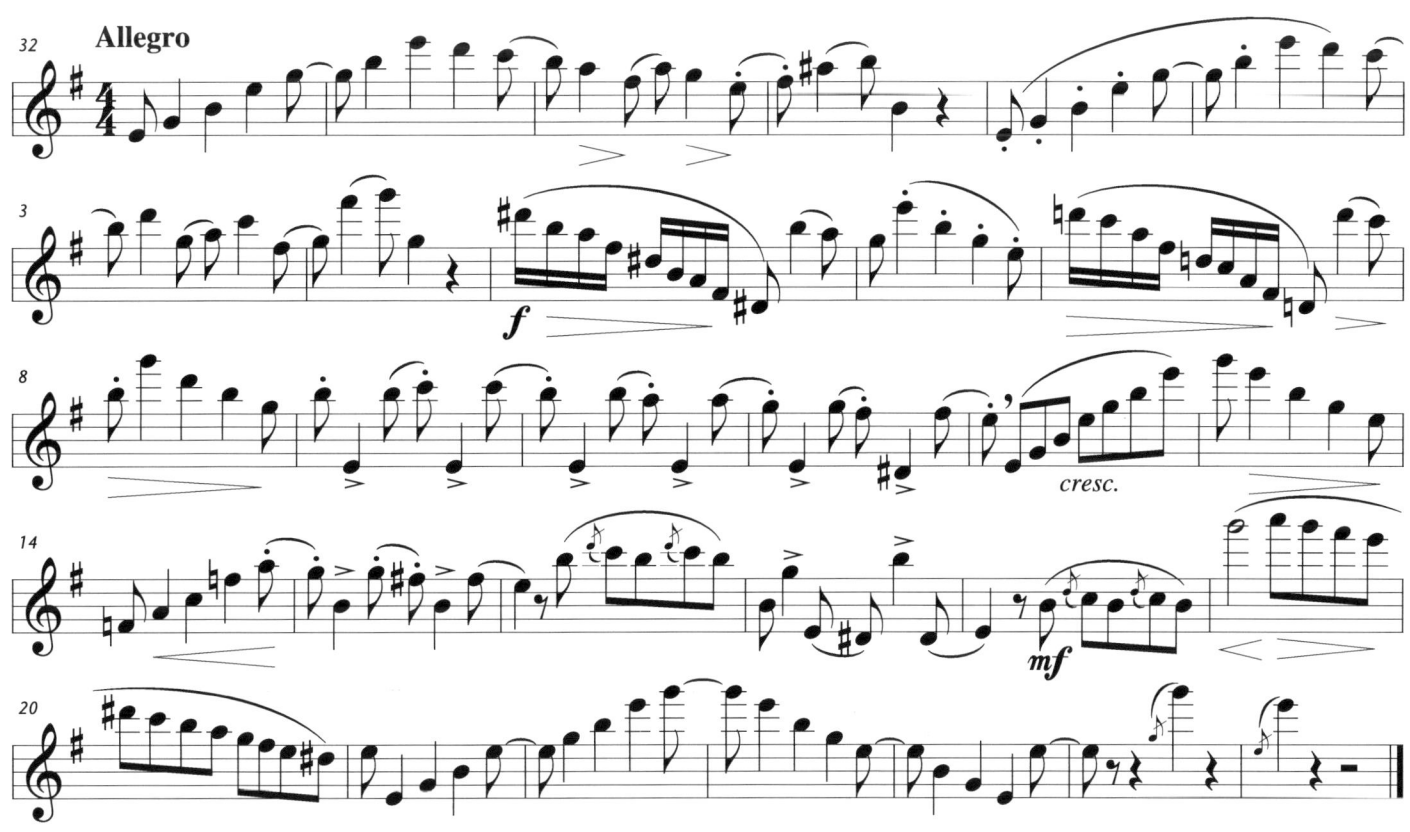

Concerto in G Major – 2nd Movement

Piano – page 48

J. J. Quantz

*) In original these passages are 1 octave lower.
   Im Original sind diese Abschnitte 1 Oktave tiefer.

Violin Concerto – 3rd Movement

L. v. Beethoven
Arr.: R. W.

Étude

E. Köhler

Allegretto

Morceau de Concours

Piano – page 66

G. Fauré

Adagio non troppo

Cool Carmen

Piano – page 58

G. Bizet

Arr.: R. Winn

Andantino quasi Allegretto
pp
p
p
dim.
pp
niente

Étude

E. Köhler

Allegro moderato
mf

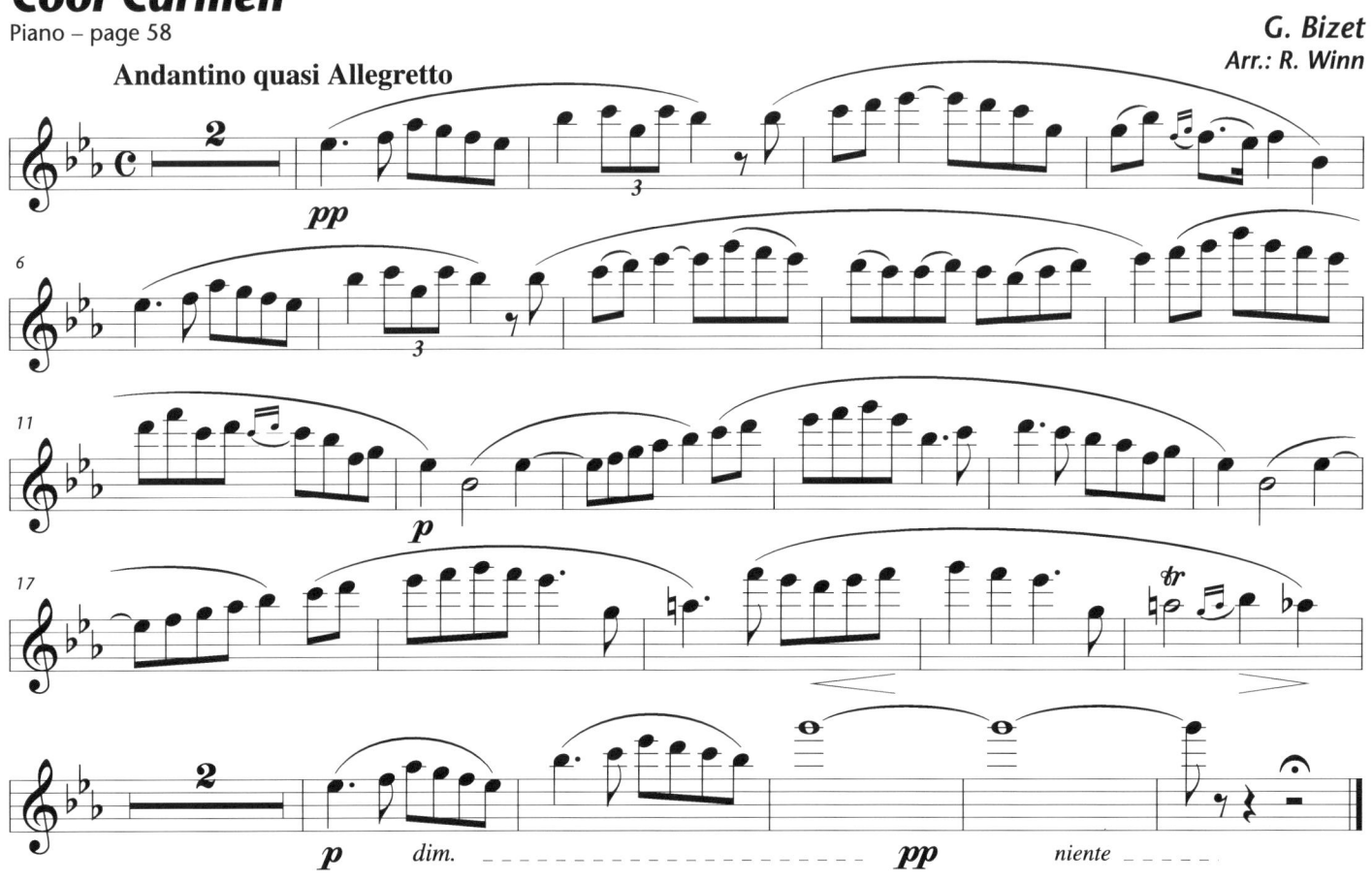

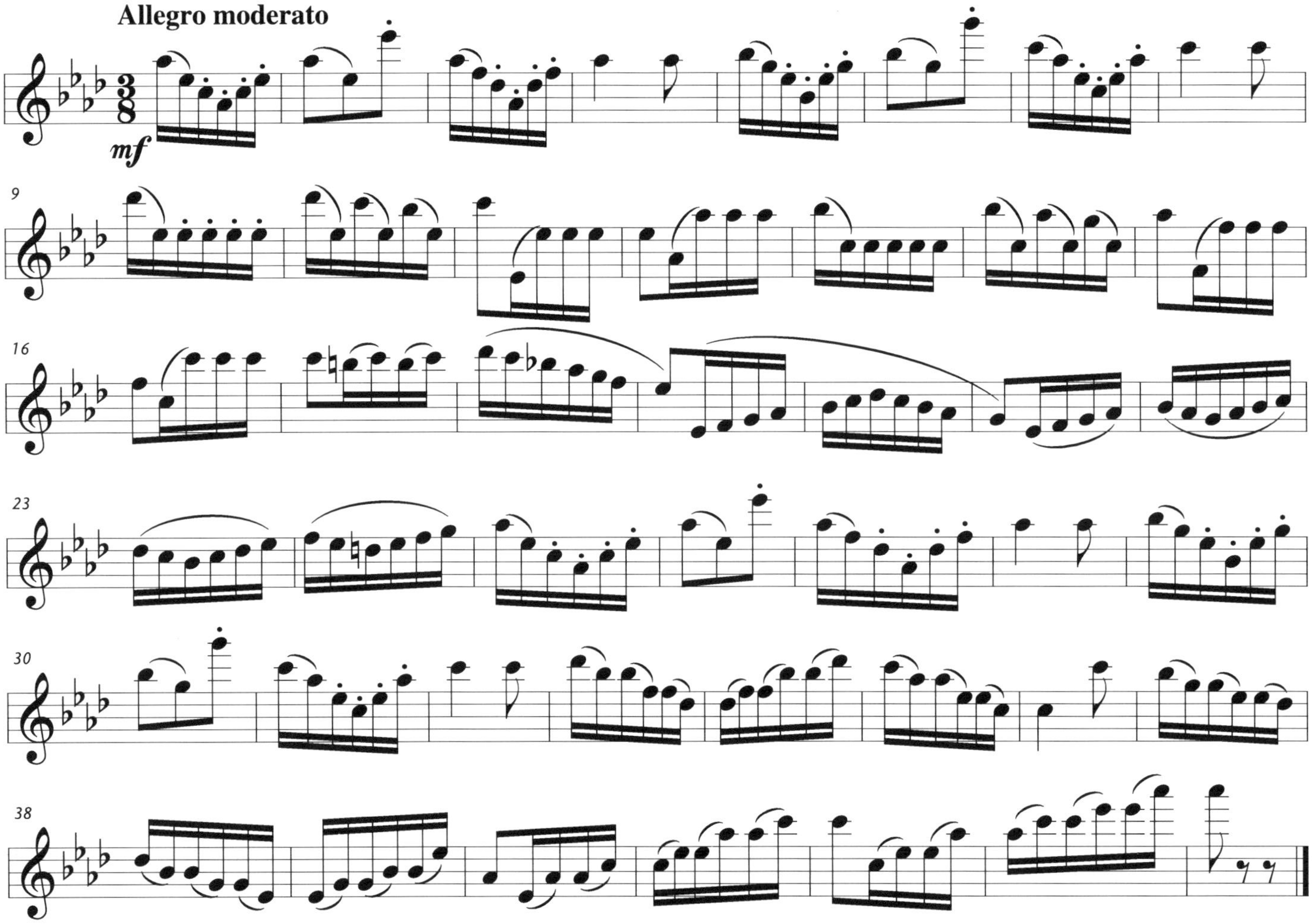

Le chant du vent

J. Donjon

Sonata in G Major

Piano – page 90

G. F. Händel (Op. 1, No. 5)

Bassoon Sonata – 2nd Movement

Piano – page 83

C. Saint-Saëns (Op. 168)

Arr.: R. W.

p
pp

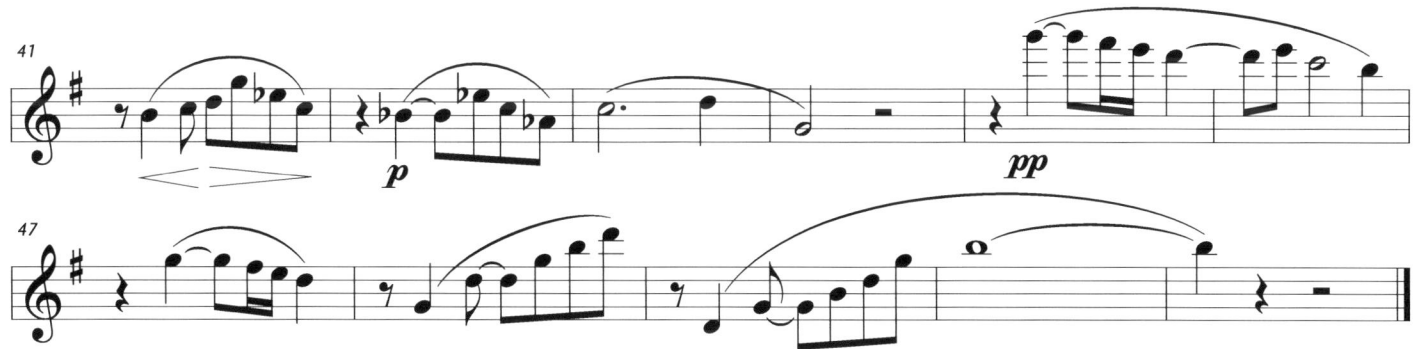

Étude

L. Drouet (72, No. 22)

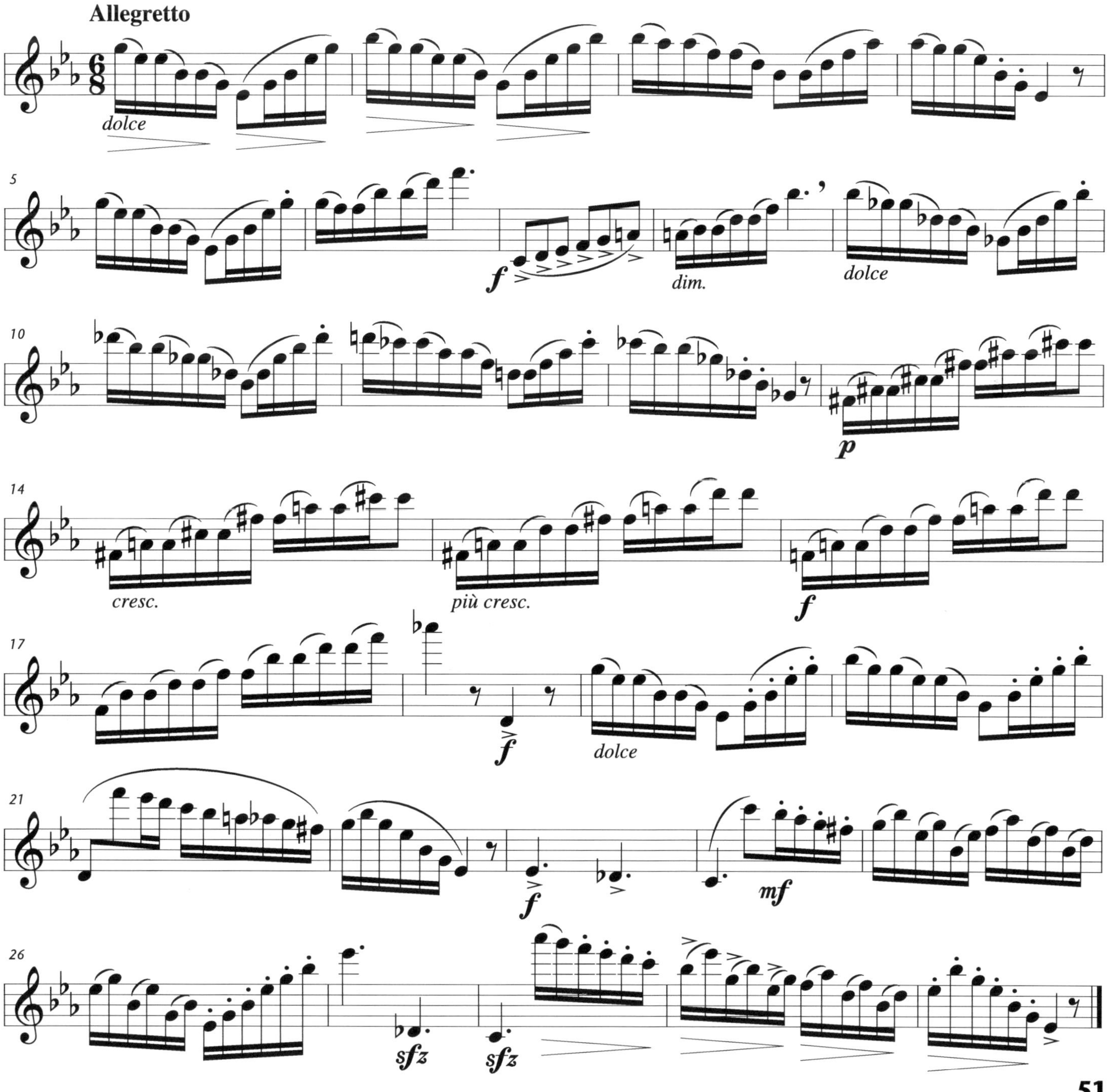
Allegretto
dolce
f
dim.
dolce
p
cresc.
più cresc.
f
f
dolce
f
mf
sfz
sfz

Andante

Piano – page 6

W. A. Mozart (KV 315)
Arr.: R. Winn

*) Cadenza by Th. Boehm

Grande Polonaise

Duos

Th. Boehm
Arr.: R.Winn

Étude

E. Köhler (Op. 33, No. 2)

Allegretto energico

Allegretto

Piano – page 40

B. Godard (Op. 116)

Étude

L. Drouet (25, No. 2)

Étude

L. Drouet (25, No. 15)

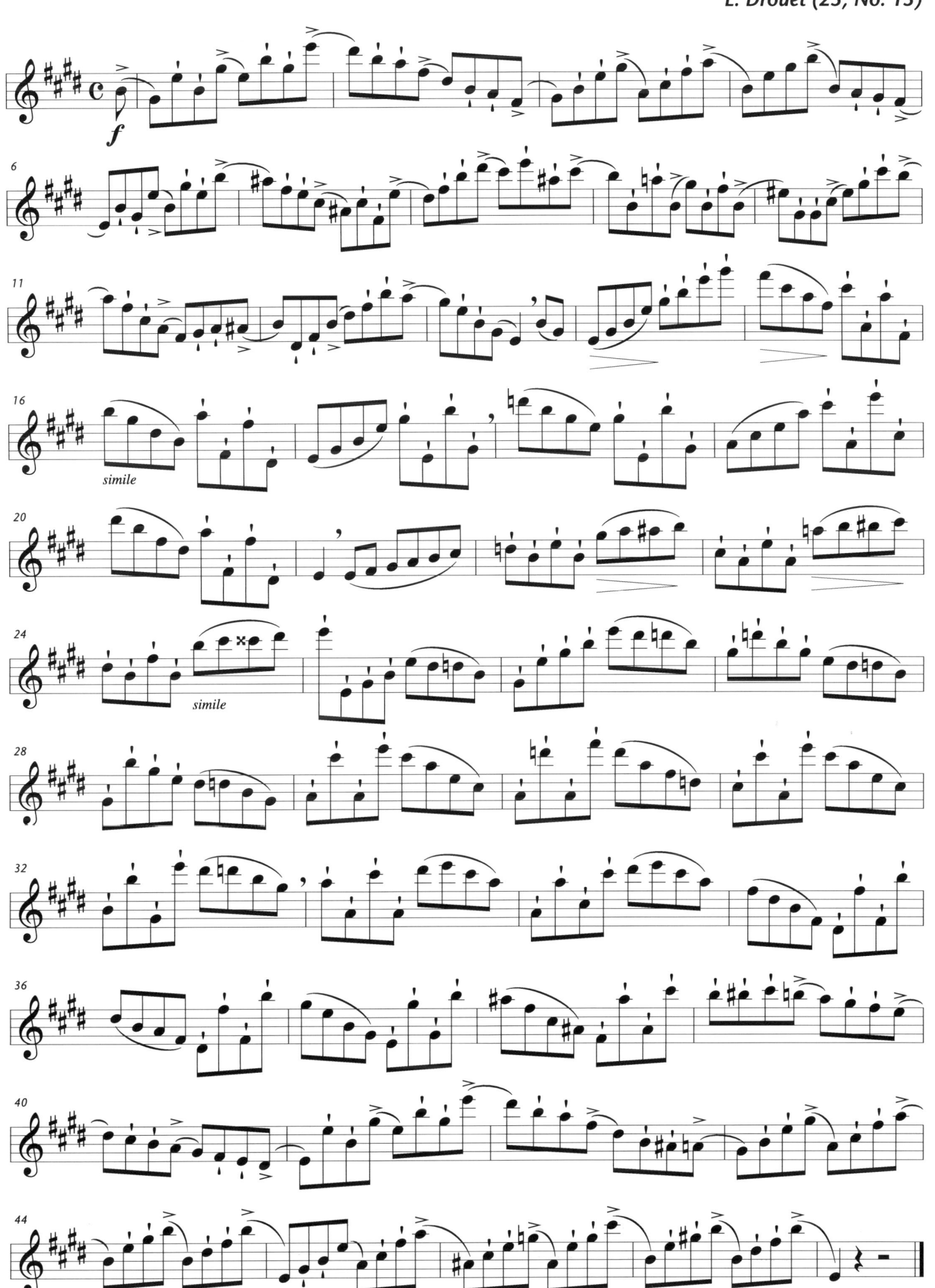

Sonata No. IV

Piano – page 78

M. Blavet

La Lumagne

Adagio

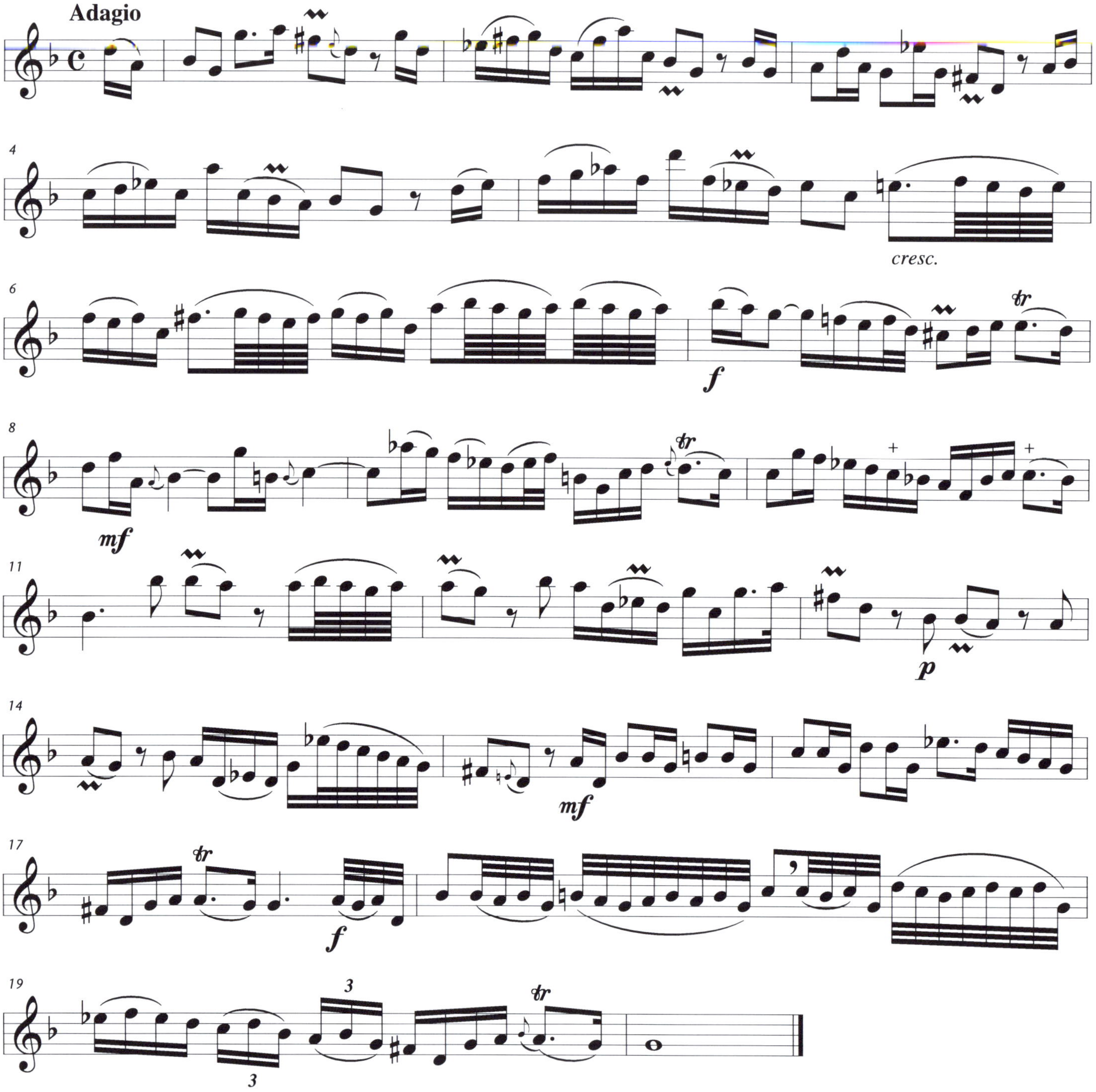

Allemanda

Allegro

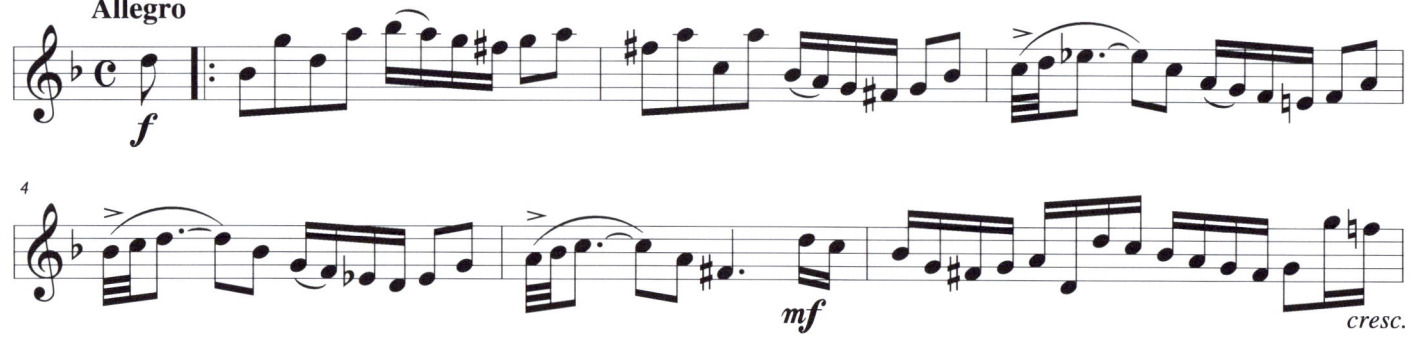

Idylle

Piano – page 43

B. Godard (Op. 116)

Quasi Adagio, molto tranquillo

62

Étude

J. Andersen (Op. 30, No. 11)

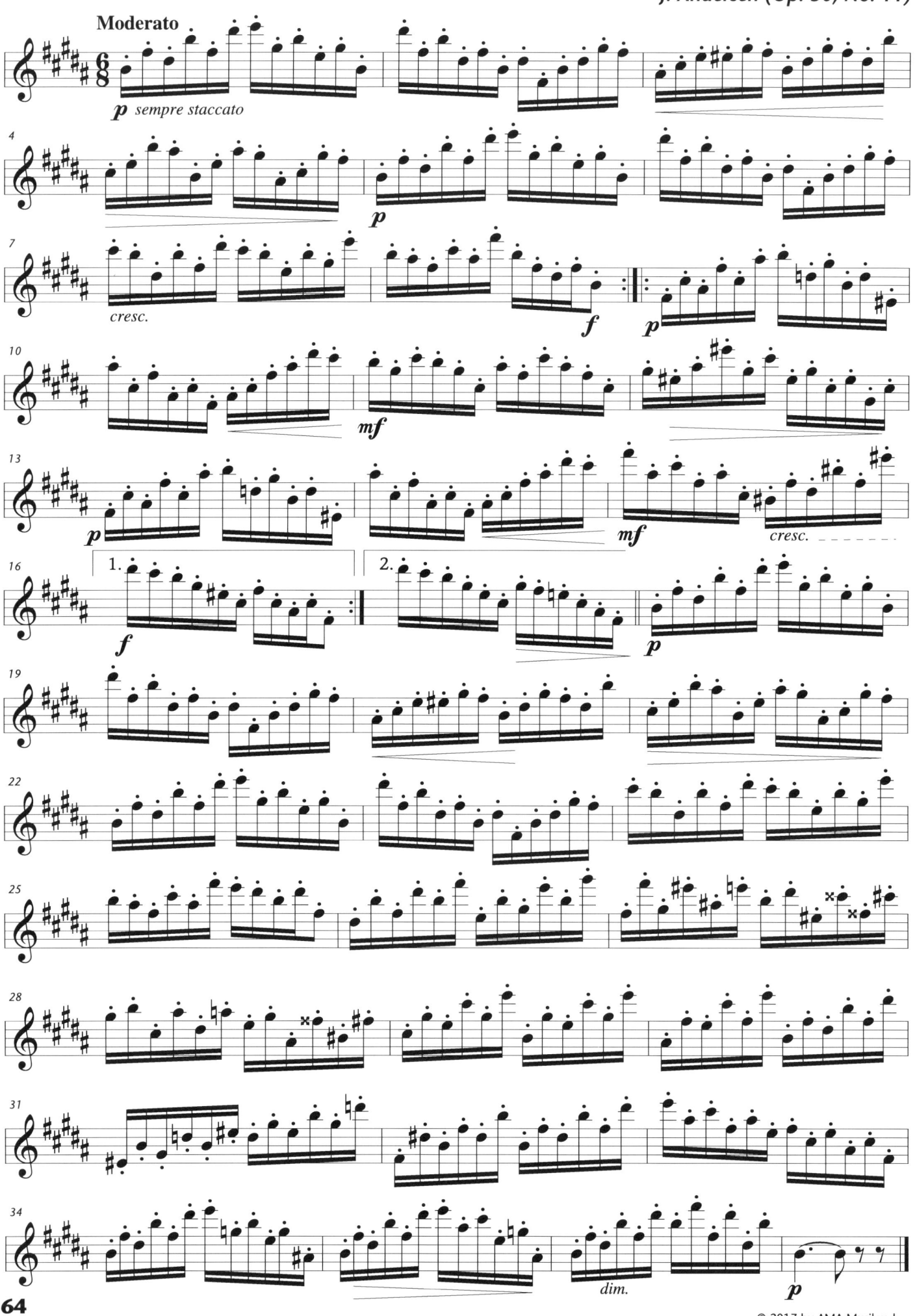

Étude

J. Andersen (Op. 30, No. 8)

Presto ma non troppo

Sonata A Minor

C. Ph. E. Bach (Wq 132)

*) A short cadenza is played here.
An dieser Stelle wird eine kurze Kadenz gespielt.

Syrinx
(La flûte de Pan)

C. Debussy (1862–1918, comp. 1913)

Scherzo
Piano – page 28

Ch. M. Widor (Op. 34, No. 2)

75

CD Content / CD-Inhalt

A German Minuet (V. Roeser)

Allegretto in B♭ (E. Köhler)

Allegro (F. A. Boieldieu)

Allegro (W. A. Mozart)

Annen-Polka (Joh. Strauss)

Badinerie – from Suite B Minor (J. S. Bach, Arr.: R. Winn)

Con Grazia (E. Köhler)

Concerto in G Major – 1st Movement (G. B. Pergolesi, Arr.: R. Winn)

Duo (A. B. Fürstenau)

Entry of the Gladiators (J. Fucik, Arr.: R. Winn)

Folk Dance: Freut euch des Lebens (E. Köhler)

Für Elise (L. v. Beethoven, Arr.: R. Winn)

German Song – nach: Kommt ein Vogel geflogen (E. Köhler)

Larghetto in Canon (W. F. Bach)

Largo (V. Bellini, Arr.: E. Köhler)

Mazurka (F. Chopin, Arr.: E. Köhler)

Moderato (E. Köhler)

Moderato in C Major (E. Köhler)

Non più andrai: Marriage of Figaro (W. A. Mozart, Arr.: R. Winn)

Operatic Melody (G. Donizetti)

Opus 75 No. 2 (W. A. Mozart)

Sonata in F Major (C. Tessarini, Arr.: R. Winn)

Sonata in G Minor (G. Ph. Telemann)

Valse - Flute (B. Godard)

Valse - Piano (B. Godard)